That Patchwork Place®

All-Star SAMPLER

Roxanne Carter

ACKNOWLEDGMENTS

I would like to thank my husband and best friend, Rob, for his patience and understanding; the people at That Patchwork Place for their encouragement; and especially my students for helping to test my instructions. I also would like to give a special thanks to Sharyn Squier Craig for teaching me all about stars.

CREDITS

Editor-in-Chief	Barbara Weiland
Technical Editor	Ursula Reikes
Managing Editor	Greg Sharp
Copy Editor	Liz McGehee
Proofreader	Leslie Phillips
Design Director	Judy Petry
Text Designer	Dani Ritchardson
Production Assistant	Shean Bemis
Illustrators	Laurel Strand
	Carolyn Kraft
Illustration Assistant	Lisa McKenney
Photographer	Brent Kane
Photographer's Assistant	Richard Lipshay

All-Star Sampler
© 1995 by Roxanne Carter
That Patchwork Place, Inc., PO Box 118, Bothell, WA 98041-0118 USA

Printed in the United States of America
00 99 98 97 96 95   6 5 4 3 2 1

Library of Congress Cataloging-in-Publication Data

Carter, Roxanne
    All-star sampler / Roxanne Carter.
        p.   cm.
    ISBN 1-56477-112-1
    1. Patchwork—Patterns. 2. Patchwork quilts.   I. Title.
TT835.C389 1995
746.46—dc20   95-18283
                                                                                    CIP

MISSION STATEMENT

WE ARE DEDICATED TO PROVIDING QUALITY PRODUCTS THAT ENCOURAGE CREATIVITY AND PROMOTE SELF-ESTEEM IN OUR CUSTOMERS AND OUR EMPLOYEES.

WE STRIVE TO MAKE A DIFFERENCE IN THE LIVES WE TOUCH.

That Patchwork Place is an employee-owned, financially secure company.

Front Cover

Stars Galore Medallion *by Roxanne Carter, 1994, Mukilteo, Washington, 72" x 72". This quilt was designed as a class sample to teach the star blocks.*

Back Cover

Left: ***Midnight Stars*** *by Debbie Stanley, 1994, Edmonds, Washington, 63" x 84". Debbie made two quilts in class; she's keeping this one. Machine pieced and quilted.*

Right: ***David's Stars*** *by Yvonne Haines, 1992, Marysville, Washington, 63" x 84". Yvonne made this quilt to hang in her husband's office. Machine pieced and hand quilted.*

TABLE OF CONTENTS

INTRODUCTION

Star blocks have always been among my favorite blocks. I seem to be drawn to quilts with star blocks in them. Several years ago, in a Star Power class taught by Sharyn Squier Craig, I learned how to draft and construct star blocks by breaking the block down into smaller units. Today, I teach others how easily star blocks can be constructed using these methods.

Directions are provided for fourteen different 12" star blocks and two different settings for assembling your blocks. The larger quilt has twelve star blocks surrounding a thirteenth block set in a center medallion. The smaller quilt has eight star blocks set on point.

GENERAL DIRECTIONS

Read through the following directions before starting your quilt. If you are unfamiliar with rotary cutting and basic strip-piecing techniques, refer to *Shortcuts: A Concise Guide to Rotary Cutting* by Donna Lynn Thomas. It contains detailed instructions for rotary cutting a variety of commonly used patchwork shapes without templates.

CUTTING DIAMONDS AND PARALLELOGRAMS

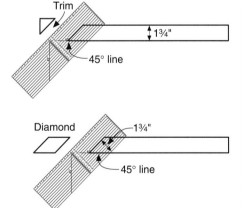

1. Cut strips from selected fabrics in the width indicated for the block you are making.

2. Cut the diamonds the same width as the width of the strips. Place the ruler's 45° line on the edge of the strip. Trim the selvage end of the strips at a 45° angle. To cut the diamonds, place the ruler's 45°-angle line at the edge of the strip and the required measurement on your ruler at the cut edge of the strip. If the strip width is 1¾", cut the diamonds 1¾" wide.

3. For parallelograms, cut segments wider than the strip width.

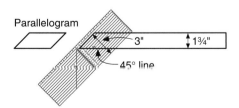

CUTTING TEMPLATE-FREE® TRIANGLES

Half-square triangles and quarter-square triangles are easy to cut from squares without the use of templates.

- For half-square triangles, cut squares the size required for the block you are making, then cut the squares once diagonally.

- For quarter-square triangles, cut squares the size required for the block you are making, then cut the squares twice diagonally.

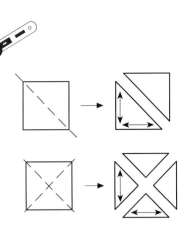

USING CUTTING GUIDES

The Castle Keep and Star of the East blocks have cutting guides to make cutting the required shapes easier. The Star of Bethlehem requires a cutoff guide to remove the corners from a rectangle. These guides can be found on page 43.

1. Trace the required cutting guide onto a piece of paper, marking the seam lines and other markings on the tracing.
2. Cut out the paper template and tape it to the underside of your ruler. Position the template on the ruler as indicated in the directions for the block you are making.
3. Position the ruler on the fabric and cut as instructed, rolling your rotary cutter along the edge of the ruler.

USING A FLANNEL BOARD

Several of the blocks use the same pieces. It is a lot of fun, as well as educational, to see how well the colors work together.

To make a flannel board, cut a piece of hardboard or heavy cardboard approximately 16" square and cover it with white flannel or fleece; just tape the flannel to the back of the board. White flannel is the best color to use so that you are not adding another color to the blocks you are laying out.

Arrange the pieces for your blocks on the flannel board, trying different color combinations. Some of the fabrics may not work as well together as others, and this is a great way to find out before sewing the blocks together. When you have decided on the color combination for each block, it is time to mark the ¼" marks on the pieces.

USING THE ¼" MARKING TEMPLATE

Make a marking template to mark the ¼" seam intersections on your pieces. Use these marks to help you match and stitch accurate points and seams.

1. Trace the marking template on page 43 onto heavy card stock or template plastic. Cut out the template.
2. Place a ruler on the edge of the template and mark the ¼" seam lines on each side of the template. Make a small hole where the lines intersect. Use a ⅛" hole punch, available from an office-supply store, or the end of an awl to make the holes.

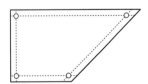

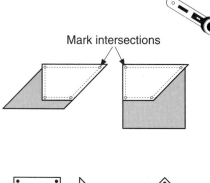

Mark intersections

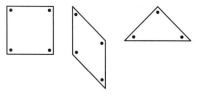

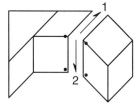

3. Use the 45°-angle point to mark the tips of diamonds and the tips of triangles. Use the wide angle on the template to mark the sides of the diamonds.
4. Use the square corner of the template to mark the corners on squares.

SEWING SET-IN SEAMS

Most of the star blocks have some pieces that can only be added by sewing the piece into a corner. Mark the intersections of all pieces following the directions above. Use a pin to match the ¼" marks at each corner when joining pieces. Follow the piecing diagram to stitch the pieces together. The ¼" marks are indicated in the illustrations with a dot.

A small dot on the piece indicates the point to start stitching and the arrow indicates the direction to stitch. If there is no dot at the other end of the piece, continue stitching all the way to the edge.

A small dot at both ends of a piece indicates that you need to stitch from mark to mark. Do not stitch beyond the marks.

The number next to the arrow between pieces indicates the order in which to sew the seams. Always start with seam 1.

Note: Always backstitch when you start or stop a seam at a ¼" mark.

CONSTRUCTING AN EIGHT-POINTED (LE MOYNE) STAR

The simplest way to construct a Le Moyne Star is to attach the background pieces to the diamond-shaped pieces first, then sew the star pieces to each other. As you sew the pieces together, you will notice that the seams must turn a corner where the background pieces meet the star pieces. This is called a set-in seam. To do this accurately, you must first mark the ¼" intersections on all diamonds, squares, and triangles. Then start and stop stitching at the ¼" marks on the pieces as indicated in the piecing diagrams.

To make the diamond units, each consisting of two diamonds and one triangle:

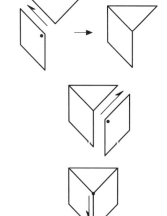

1. Sew a triangle to a diamond. Use a pin to match the ¼" marks on each of the two pieces. Begin stitching at the ¼" mark; backstitch. Stitch in the direction of the arrow all the way to the outer edge.

2. Sew a second diamond to the triangle, starting at the ¼" mark on the inner point; backstitch. Stitch in the direction of the arrow to the outer edge.

3. Match the points of the diamonds and sew them together, starting at the inner ¼" mark. Press this seam to one side and press the seams on the triangle toward the diamonds.

To add a square between two diamond units:
1. Sew a square to a diamond unit. Begin stitching at the ¼" mark; backstitch. Stitch in the direction of the arrow all the way to the outer edge.

2. Sew a second diamond unit to the square. Begin stitching at the ¼" mark; backstitch. Stitch in the direction of the arrow all the way to the outer edge.

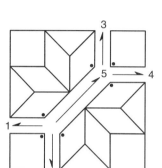

3. Match the points of the diamonds and sew them together, starting at the inner ¼" mark. Press this seam to one side and press the seams on the square toward the diamonds.

To assemble the block:
1. Sew the sides of the large diamond units to adjacent sides of one square. Begin stitching at the ¼" mark; backstitch. Stitch in the direction of the arrow all the way to the outer edge. Repeat with the remaining square.
2. Match the center points and pin.
3. Stitch from mark to mark. Press the center seam to one side and press the seams of the squares toward the diamonds.

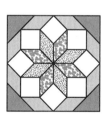

THE QUILTS

The first step is to decide which quilt setting you want to make. The second step is to decide which blocks you want to make for the setting you have chosen. The third step is to select your fabrics. Before selecting your fabrics, study the color photographs of the quilts in the Gallery to see what a difference color placement can make in the final appearance of each block and in the entire quilt. The Rolling Star blocks shown at right illustrate how different fabric color placements can change the entire look of a block.

I suggest choosing a main fabric to use predominately throughout the blocks, four other prints or tone-on-tone fabrics that go well with the main fabric, and a neutral background fabric that blends well with all the fabrics.

The directions for each block include the size of the pieces and the number of pieces to cut. Each piece is labeled with a letter for easy reference to the cutting directions and the piecing diagram. Most of the pieces for the blocks are rotary cut; however, a few require the use of a cutting guide. Refer to the directions on page 5 for using cutting guides.

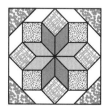

Yardage Requirements for Stars Galore Medallion

Finished Size: 72" x 72"
Materials: 44"-wide fabric

Blocks (See Color Key on page 9.)
   1 yd. each of 4 different
      fabrics (Fabrics #1, #2,
      #3, #4)
   1 yd. main fabric (Fabric #5)
   1 yd. background (Fabric #6)

Center Background
   ½ yd.

Sashing
   1 yd. for sashing strips
   ¼ yd. for cornerstones

Inner Border
   ½ yd.

Middle Pieced Border
   ¾ yd. light background
   ¾ yd. medium background
   ½ yd. diamond #1
   ½ yd. diamond #2

Outer Border
   1 yd.

Backing
   4½ yds.

Binding
   ⅝ yd.

Yardage Requirements for Eight Stars on Point

Block Color Key

▢	Fabric 1: Light purple print
▢	Fabric 2: Dark purple print
▢	Fabric 3: Green print
▢	Fabric 4: Blue print
▢	Fabric 5: Multicolor print (main fabric)
▢	Fabric 6: Background

Finished Size: 63" x 84"
Materials: 44"-wide fabric

Blocks
⅝ yd. each of 4 different fabrics (Fabrics #1, #2, #3, #4)
⅝ yd. main fabric (Fabric #5)
¾ yd. background (Fabric #6)

Sashing
¾ yd. for sashing strips
¼ yd. for cornerstones

Setting Triangles
1 yd.

Inner Border
¾ yd.

Middle Pieced Border
¾ yd. light background
¾ yd. medium background
½ yd. diamond #1
½ yd. diamond #2

Outer Border
¾ yd.

Backing
4 yds.

Binding
⅝ yd.

THE STAR BLOCKS

DUTCH ROSE

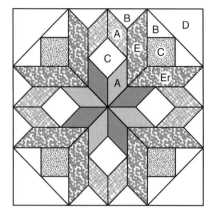

Cutting

Cut diamonds from strips, following directions on page 4.

Fabric	Piece	Cut
1	A	4 diamonds from 1¾"-wide strips
2	A	4 diamonds from 1¾"-wide strips
3	A	8 diamonds from 1¾"-wide strips
4	C	4 squares, each 2¼" x 2¼"
5	E	1 strip, 1¾" x 42"; fold strip in half, wrong sides together. Cut 4 segments, each 3" wide, at a 45° angle, following directions on page 4. You will get 4 Piece E and 4 reverse Piece E.
6	B	4 squares, each 3¾" x 3¾"; cut twice diagonally for 16 quarter-square triangles.
	C	4 squares, each 2¼" x 2¼"
	D	2 squares, each 4⅜" x 4⅜"; cut once diagonally for 4 half-square triangles.

Piecing

Mark the ¼" seam intersections on all pieces. Matching the ¼" marks, sew the pieces together in numerical order. Stitch from the marks in the direction of the arrows as indicated in the illustrations.

Center Units

1. Sew a Fabric #1 and a Fabric #2 diamond (A) to the sides of a 2¼" background square (C). Match the points of the diamonds and stitch. Trim the tips of the diamonds that extend beyond the seam allowance. Press the seams of the diamonds to one side, and the seams of the square toward the diamonds. Press the seams of the diamonds in the same direction around the block.

2. Sew two Fabric #3 diamonds to the remaining sides of the background square (C) in the same manner to complete the center unit.

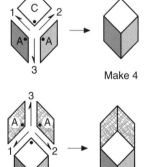

Center Unit
Make 4

Corner Units

1. Sew the short sides of 2 small background triangles (B) to the sides of a 2¼" Fabric #4 square (C). Sew this unit to a large background triangle ((D). Press the seam allowances toward the large triangle.

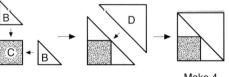

Make 4

2. Sew a Fabric #5 parallelogram (E) to one side of the corner unit. Repeat with a reverse parallelogram (E reverse) on the other side of the corner unit. Match the points of the parallelogram and stitch. Trim the tips of the parallelogram extending beyond the seam allowances and press the seam allowances to one side.

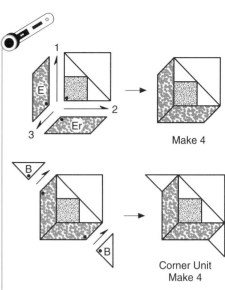

Make 4

3. Sew the short side of a small background triangle (B) to the end of each parallelogram (E) to complete the corner unit.

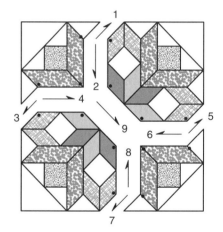

Corner Unit
Make 4

Block Assembly

1. Sew the center units to the sides of a corner unit.

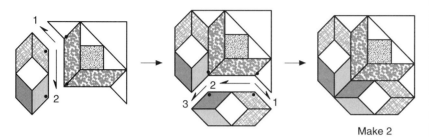

Make 2

2. Sew the units together as shown to complete the block. Stitch the seams in numerical order. If the seam allowances of the diamonds were pressed in the same direction, they will butt together easily, creating a nice, clean join.

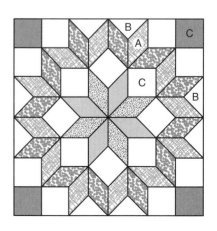

CARPENTER'S WHEEL

Cutting

Cut diamonds from strips, following directions on page 4.

Fabric	Piece	Cut
1	A	4 diamonds from 1¾"-wide strips
2	C	4 squares, each 2¼" x 2¼"
3	A	12 diamonds from 1¾"-wide strips
4	A	4 diamonds from 1¾"-wide strips
5	A	12 diamonds from 1¾"-wide strips
6	B	2 squares, each 3¾" x 3¾"; cut twice diagonally for quarter-square triangles
	C	16 squares, each 2¼" x 2¼"

Piecing

Mark the ¼" seam intersections on all pieces. Matching the ¼" marks, sew the pieces together in numerical order. Stitch from the marks in the direction of the arrows as indicated in the illustrations.

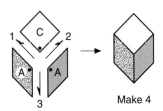

Make 4

Center Units

1. Sew a Fabric #1 and a Fabric #4 diamond (A) to the sides of a 2¼" background square (C). Match the points of the diamonds and stitch. Trim the tips of the diamonds that extend beyond the seam allowances. Press the seams of the diamonds to one side, and the seams of the square toward the diamonds. Press the seams of the diamonds in the same direction around the block.

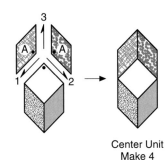

Center Unit
Make 4

2. Sew a Fabric #3 and a Fabric #5 diamond (A) to the opposite side of the background square (C) in the same manner to complete the center unit.

Corner Units

1. Sew a Fabric #3 and a Fabric #5 diamond (A) to the sides of a 2¼" background square (C). Match the points of the diamonds (A) and stitch. Trim the tips of the diamonds that extend beyond the seam allowances. Press the seams of the diamonds to one side and the seams of the square toward the diamonds.

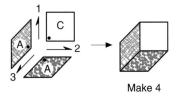

Make 4

2. Sew a Fabric #5 diamond (A) to the side of a 2¼" background square (C). Sew this unit to the left side of the unit made in step 1. Press the seams of the diamond to one side and the seams of the square toward the diamonds. Trim the tips of the diamonds that extend beyond the seam allowance.

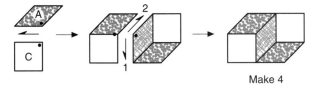

Make 4

3. Sew a 2¼" Fabric #2 square, a 2¼" background square, and a Fabric #3 diamond together. Sew this unit to the bottom of the unit made in step 2.

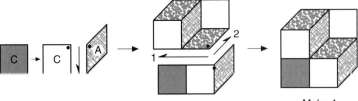

Make 4

4. Sew the short side of a small background triangle (B) to the side of each diamond to complete the corner unit.

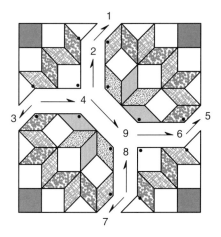

Corner Unit
Make 4

Block Assembly

1. Sew a center unit to each side of a corner unit. Press the seams of the diamonds to one side and press the seams of the square toward the diamonds. Trim off any diamond tips that extend beyond the seam allowance.

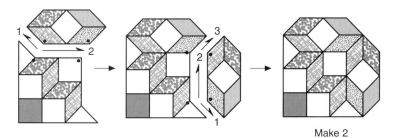

Make 2

2. Sew the units together as shown to complete the block. Stitch the seams in numerical order. If the seam allowances of the diamonds were pressed in the same direction, they will butt together easily, creating a nice, clean join.

STAR OF BETHLEHEM

Cutting

Cut diamonds from strips, following directions on page 4.

Fabric	Piece	Cut
2	A	8 diamonds from 1¾"-wide strips
3	A	4 diamonds from 1¾"-wide strips
4	A	4 diamonds from 1¾"-wide strips
5	C	8 rectangles, each 3" x 3⅝"; corners will be removed later
6	B	4 squares, each 3¾" x 3¾"; cut twice diagonally for quarter-square triangles
	D	2 squares, each 4⅜" x 4⅜"; cut once diagonally for half-square triangles

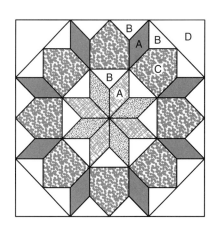

Piecing

Mark the ¼" seam intersections on all pieces. Matching the ¼" marks, sew the pieces together in numerical order. Stitch from the marks in the direction of the arrows as indicated in the illustrations.

Center Units

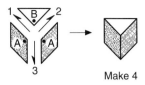

Make 4

1. Sew a Fabric #3 and a Fabric #4 diamond (A) to the sides of a small background triangle (B). Match the points of the diamonds and stitch. Trim the tips of the diamonds that extend beyond the seam allowances. Press the seams of the diamonds to one side and the seams of the triangle toward the diamonds. Press the seams of the diamonds in the same direction around the block.

2. Make a paper template of the cutoff guide on page 43. Align the long edge of the template with the edge of a ruler; tape in place. Place the template on one corner of a Fabric #5 rectangle (C). Trim; repeat with the other corner to make Piece C.

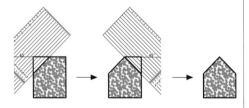

Cut 8

3. Sew Piece C to the unit made in step 1.

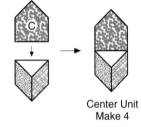

Center Unit
Make 4

Corner Units

Make 4

1. Sew the long edge of a background triangle (B) to the bottom edge of the remaining Piece C.

2. Sew a Fabric #2 diamond (A) and background triangle (B) together. Sew this unit to the side of the unit made in step 1. Add a Fabric #2 diamond and a background triangle to the other side of the unit in the same manner. Notice the orientation of the triangle and diamond before you stitch them together. Press the seams toward the diamonds. Trim the diamond tips that extend beyond the seam allowances.

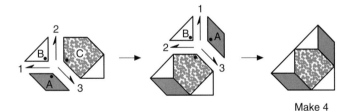

Make 4

3. Sew a large background triangle (D) to the top of the unit made in step 2. Add a small background triangle (B) to each side.

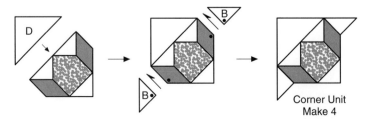

Corner Unit
Make 4

Block Assembly

1. Sew the center units to the sides of a corner unit.

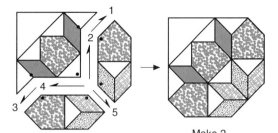

Make 2

2. Sew the units together as shown to complete the block. Stitch the seams in numerical order. If the seam allowances of the diamonds were pressed in the same direction, they will butt together easily, creating a nice, clean join.

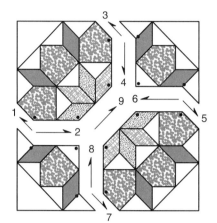

SNOW CRYSTAL

Cutting

Cut diamonds from strips, following directions on page 4.

Fabric	Piece	Cut
1	A	8 diamonds from 1¾"-wide strips
2	A	8 diamonds from 1¾"-wide strips
3	A	8 diamonds from 1¾"-wide strips
4	A	4 diamonds from 1¾"-wide strips
5	A	4 diamonds from 1¾"-wide strips
6	B	2 squares, each 3¾" x 3¾"; cut twice diagonally for quarter-square triangles
	C	12 squares, each 2¼" x 2¼"
	D	4 rectangles, each 2¼" x 4"

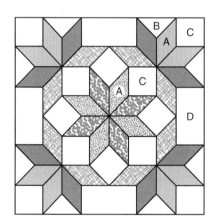

Piecing

Mark the ¼" seam intersections on all pieces. Matching the ¼" marks, sew the pieces together in numerical order. Stitch from the marks in the direction of the arrows as indicated in the illustrations.

Corner Units

1. Sew a Fabric #1 and a Fabric #2 diamond (A) to the sides of a small background triangle (B). Match the points of the diamonds and stitch. Trim the tips of the diamonds that extend beyond the seam allowances. Press the seams of the diamonds to one side and the seams of the triangle toward the diamonds. Press the seams of the diamonds in the same direction around the block. Make 4 of each color combination for a total of 8.

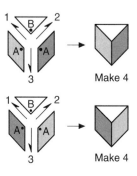

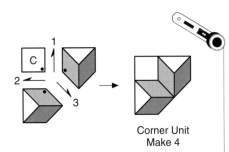

Corner Unit
Make 4

2. Sew a 2¼" background square (C) between 2 units made in step 1. Use one of each color combination, placing the Fabric #1 diamonds next to each other.

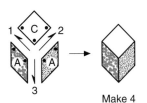

Make 4

Center Unit

1. Sew a Fabric #4 and a Fabric #5 diamond (A) to the sides of a 2¼" background square (C). Match the points of the diamonds and stitch. Trim the tips of the diamonds that extend beyond the seam allowances. Press the seams of the diamonds to one side and the seams of the square toward the diamonds. Press the seams of the diamonds in the same direction around the block.

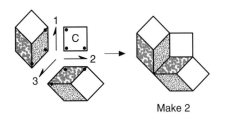

Make 2

2. Sew a 2¼" background square (C) between 2 units made in step 1.

3. Sew two 2¼" background squares (C) between the units made in step 2, then stitch the center seam.

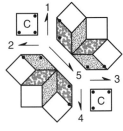

Center Unit

Block Assembly

1. Sew the Fabric #3 diamonds (A) to the center unit. Place the diamonds on top and stitch from the ¼" mark to the outer edge.

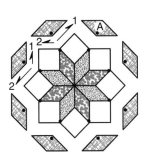

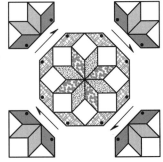

2. Sew the corner units to the center unit.

3. Insert the background rectangles (D). Stitch the long side first, then the two short sides.

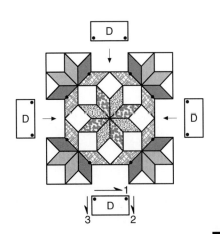

ROLLING STAR

Cutting

Cut diamonds from strips, following directions on page 4.

Fabric	Piece	Cut
1	C	4 squares, each 3" x 3"
2	B	4 diamonds from 2¼"-wide strips
3	B	8 diamonds from 2¼"-wide strips
5	B	4 diamonds from 2¼"-wide strips
6	A	2 squares, each 4⅜" x 4⅜"; cut once diagonally for half-square triangles
	C	4 squares, each 3" x 3"

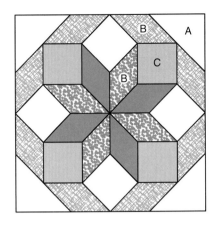

Piecing

Mark the ¼" seam intersections on all pieces. Matching the ¼" marks, sew the pieces together in numerical order. Stitch from the marks in the direction of the arrows as indicated in the illustrations.

Center Units

Sew a Fabric #2 and a Fabric #5 diamond (B) to the sides of a 2¼" background square (C). Match the points of the diamonds and stitch. Trim the tips of the diamonds that extend beyond the seam allowances. Press the seams of the diamonds to one side and the seams of the square toward the diamonds. Press the seams of the diamonds in the same direction around the block.

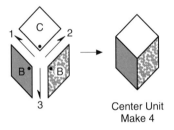

Center Unit
Make 4

Corner Units

Sew 2 Fabric #3 diamonds (B) to the sides of a 2¼" Fabric #1 square (C). Sew this unit to a large background triangle (A). Press the seams of the diamonds toward the square and the triangle. Trim the diamond tips that extend beyond the seam allowances.

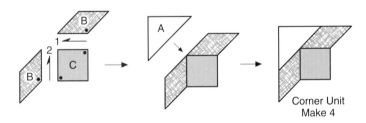

Corner Unit
Make 4

Block Assembly

1. Sew the center units to the sides of a corner unit.

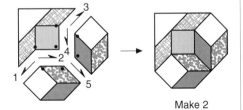

Make 2

2. Sew the units together as shown to complete the block. Stitch the seams in numerical order.

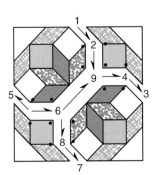

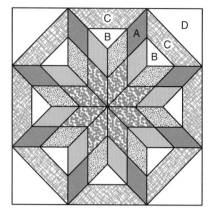

BLAZING STAR

Cutting

Cut diamonds from strips, following directions on page 4.

Fabric		Piece	Cut	
1	⬜	A	1 strip, 1¾" x 42"	
2	⬛	A	1 strip, 1¾" x 42"	
3	⬜	C	2 squares, each 6¼" x 6¼"; cut twice diagonally for quarter-square triangles	⊠
4	⬜	A	1 strip, 1¾" x 42"	
5	⬜	A	1 strip, 1¾" x 42"	
6	⬜	B	4 squares, each 2⅝" x 2⅝"; cut once diagonally for half-square triangles	◨
		D	2 squares, 4⅜" x 4⅜"; cut once diagonally for half-square triangles	◨

Piecing

Diamond Units

1. Sew the 1¾" strips together, staggering the seams about 1" as shown, to make 2 strip units. Align the 45° line on the ruler with a horizontal seam and cut one end at a 45° angle. Cut 8 segments, 1¾" wide, from each strip unit, making each cut parallel to the first cut.

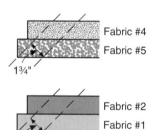

Fabric #4
Fabric #5
1¾"

Fabric #2
Fabric #1
1¾"

2. Matching the seams, sew a segment from each strip unit together to make a diamond unit.

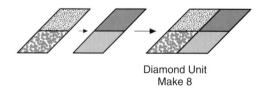

Diamond Unit
Make 8

Corner Squares

1. To make a trapezoid (C), place the ruler's 1¾" mark on the long edge of a Fabric #3 quarter-square triangle. Use a rotary cutter to trim the corner.

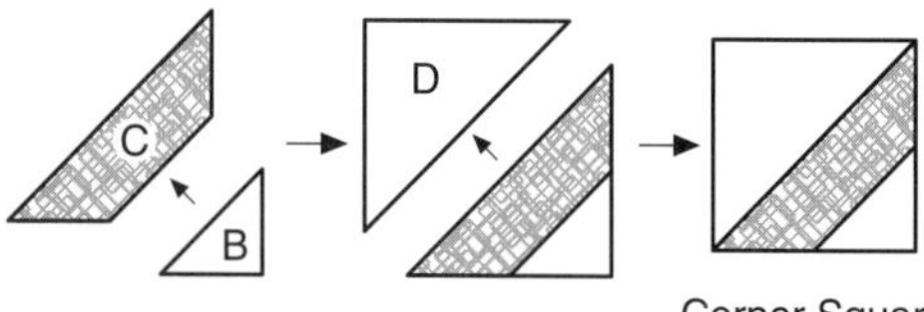

← 1¾" line

← Discard

Cut 8

2. Sew a small background triangle (B) to the short side of a Fabric #3 trapezoid (C). To each of 4 B/C units, sew a large background triangle (D) to make a corner square. Press the seams toward the trapezoid. Use the remaining 4 B/C units for the side triangles.

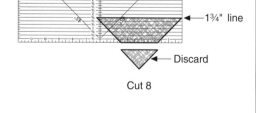

Side Triangle
Make 8

Corner Square
Make 4

Block Assembly

Arrange the diamonds, side triangles (B/C), and corner squares (B/C/D) as shown. Make all ¼" marks on the diamonds, triangles, and squares. Sew the units together, following the directions on pages 6–7 for constructing an eight-pointed star.

VIRGINIA STAR

Cutting

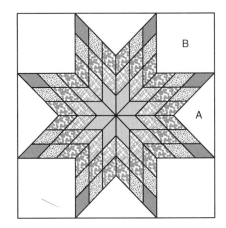

Fabric	Piece	Cut
1 ▢	—	1 strip, 1⅜" x 42"
2 ▨	—	1 strip, 1⅜" x 42"
3 ▨	—	2 strips, each 1⅜" x 42"
4 ▨	—	2 strips, each 1⅜" x 42"
5 ▨	—	3 strips, each 1⅜" x 42"
6 ▢	A	1 square, 6¼" x 6¼"; cut twice diagonally for half-square triangles
	B	4 squares, each 4" x 4"

Piecing

Diamond Units

1. Sew the 1⅜"-wide strips together, staggering the seams about 1" as shown, to make 3 different strip units. Align the 45° line on the ruler with a horizontal seam and cut one end at a 45° angle. Cut 8 segments, each 1⅜" wide, from each strip unit, making each cut parallel to the first cut.

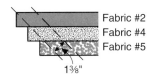
Fabric #2
Fabric #4
Fabric #5
1⅜"

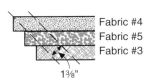
Fabric #4
Fabric #5
Fabric #3
1⅜"

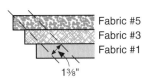
Fabric #5
Fabric #3
Fabric #1
1⅜"

2. Matching the seams, sew a segment from each unit together to make a diamond unit.

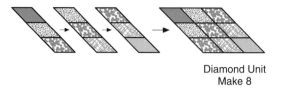

Diamond Unit
Make 8

Block Assembly

Arrange the diamond units, side triangles (A), and corner squares (B) as shown. Make all ¼" marks on the diamonds, triangles, and squares. Sew the units together, following the directions on pages 6–7 for constructing an eight-pointed star.

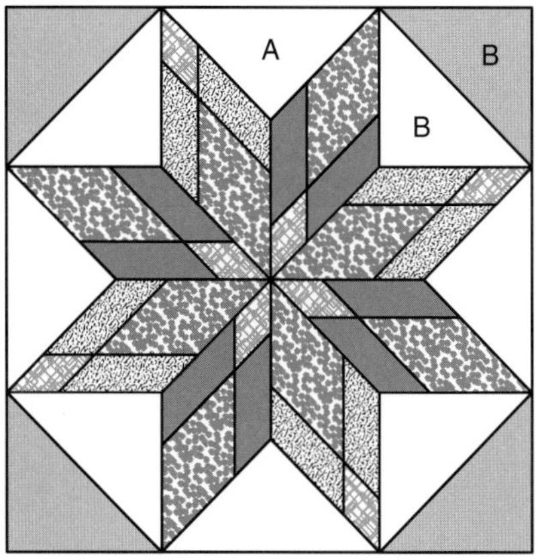

FLYING STAR

Cutting

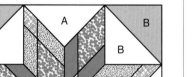

Fabric		Piece	Cut	
1		B	2 squares, each 4⅜" x 4⅜"; cut once diagonally for half-square triangles	
2		—	1 strip, 1⅜" x 22"	
		—	1 strip, 2⅛" x 22"	
3		—	2 strips, each 1⅜" x 22"	
4		—	1 strip, 1⅜" x 22"	
			1 strip, 2⅛" x 22"	
5		—	2 strips, each 2⅛" x 22"	
6		A	1 square, 6¼" x 6¼"; cut twice diagonally for quarter-square triangles	
		B	2 squares, each 4⅜" x 4⅜"; cut once diagonally for half-square triangles	

(Continued on page 25)

Eight Stars on Point by Roxanne Carter,
*1990, Mukilteo, Washington, 63" x 84". This
was my first all-star quilt, made for my
star-block class.*

Kim's Medallion by Roxanne Carter, 1994,
*Mukilteo, Washington, 26" x 26". I made
only the center medallion of the Stars
Galore Medallion quilt for this wall
hanging, which I gave to my daughter,
Kimberly Gangloff.*

Tango of Stars by Joan White, 1993, Seattle, Washington, 54" x 74". Machine pieced, hand and machine quilted.

Edmonds Stars *by Pat Mead, 1992, Edmonds, Washington, 85" x 105". Pat added two pieced borders to make a larger quilt. Machine quilted by Roxanne Carter, hand quilted by Pat Mead.*

Linda's Stars Galore by Linda Levinson,
1992, Mukilteo, Washington, 65" x 85".
Machine quilted by Patsi Hanseth.

Clearview Stars by Kay Melder, 1993,
Snohomish, Washington, 63" x 84".
Machine pieced and hand quilted.

(Flying Star continued from page 20)

Piecing

Diamond Units

1. Sew the 1⅜"- and 2⅛"-wide strips together, staggering the seams about 1" as shown, to make 4 different strip units. Align the 45° line on the ruler with a horizontal seam and cut one end at a 45° angle. Cut the following segments from the appropriate strip units. Make each cut parallel to the first cut.

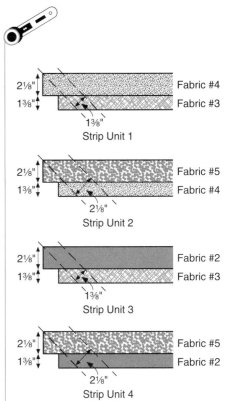

Strip Unit	No. of Segments	Width of Segments
1	4	1⅜"
2	4	2⅛"
3	4	1⅜"
4	4	2⅛"

2. Sew the 1⅜"-wide segments and 2⅛"-wide segments together as shown to make diamond units.

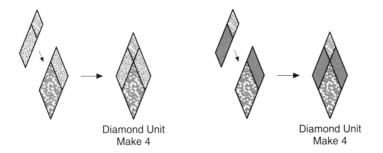

Diamond Unit
Make 4

Diamond Unit
Make 4

Corner Squares

Sew a large background triangle (B) and a Fabric #1 triangle (B) together to make the corner squares.

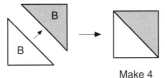

Make 4

Block Assembly

Arrange the diamond units, quarter-square triangles (A), and pieced corner squares (B/B) as shown. Make all ¼" marks on the diamonds, triangles, and squares. Sew the units together, following the directions on pages 6–7 for constructing an eight-pointed star.

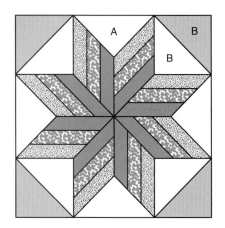

LIBERTY STAR

Cutting

Fabric		Piece	Cut	
1	◩	B	2 squares, each 4⅜" x 4⅜"; cut once diagonally for half-square triangles	◩
2	◩	—	1 strip, 1⅜" x 42"	
4	◩	—	1 strip, 1⅜" x 42"	
5	◩	—	1 strip, 1⅜" x 42"	
6	☐	A	1 square, 6¼" x 6¼"; cut twice diagonally for quarter-square triangles	⊠
		B	2 squares, each 4⅜" x 4⅜"; cut once diagonally for half-square triangles	◩

Piecing

Diamond Units

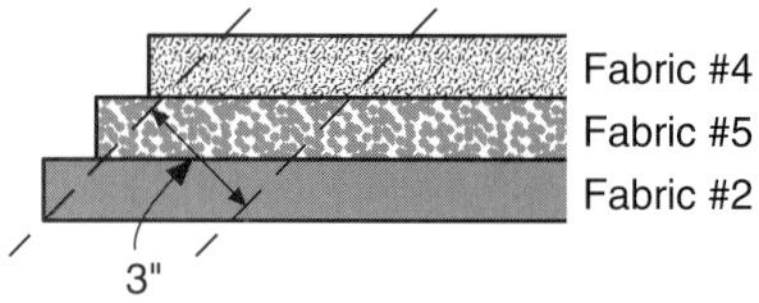

1. Sew the 1⅜"-wide strips together, staggering the seams about 1" as shown. Align the 45° line on the ruler with a horizontal seam and cut one end at a 45° angle.

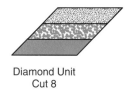

Fabric #4
Fabric #5
Fabric #2

3"

Diamond Unit
Cut 8

2. Cut 8 segments, each 3" wide, from the strip unit, making each cut parallel to the first cut.

Corner Squares

Sew a background triangle (B) and a Fabric #1 triangle (B) together to make the corner squares.

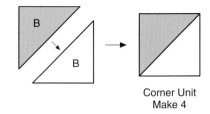

Corner Unit
Make 4

Block Assembly

Arrange the diamond units, triangles (A), and corner squares (B/B) as shown. Make all ¼" marks on the diamonds, triangles, and squares. Sew the units together, following the directions on pages 6–7 for constructing an eight-pointed star.

STAR OF THE EAST

Cutting

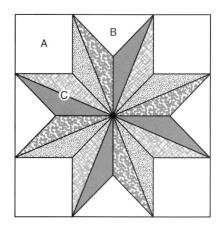

Fabric	Piece	Cut
2 ▪	—	1 strip, 2" x 42"
3 ▪	—	1 strip, 2" x 42"
4 ▪	—	1 strip, 2" x 42"
5 ▪	—	1 strip, 2" x 42"
6 ☐	A	4 squares, each 4" x 4"
	B	1 square, 6¼" x 6¼"; cut twice diagonally for half-square triangles ⊠

Piecing

Diamond Units

1. With right sides together, sew the Fabric #2 and Fabric #3 strips together on both long edges using a ¼"-wide seam allowance. Repeat with Fabric #4 and Fabric #5 strips.

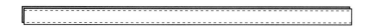

2. Make a paper template of the Star of the East cutting guide on page 43; mark the seam lines on the template (see page 5). Place one of the short sides of the template on the underside of a ruler; tape in place.

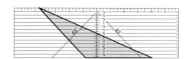

3. Place the long edge of the template on one edge of the strip unit. Cut along the edge of the ruler. Turn the cut piece over, align the short side of the template with the edge you just cut, and cut the second short side. Cut 4 half diamonds from each strip unit.

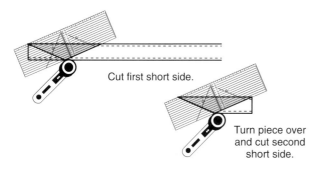

Cut first short side.

Turn piece over and cut second short side.

4. Carefully undo the stitching at the point of each piece, open up into a diamond, and press the seam open. Trim away any tips extending beyond the cut edge.

Remove stitches at point and press diamond open.

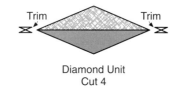

Trim   Trim

Diamond Unit
Cut 4

Block Assembly

Arrange diamond units, side triangles (B), and corner squares (A) as shown. Make all ¼" marks on the diamonds, triangles, and squares. Sew the units together, following the directions on pages 6–7 for constructing an eight-pointed star.

FLYING SWALLOWS

Cutting

Cut diamonds from strips, following directions on page 4.

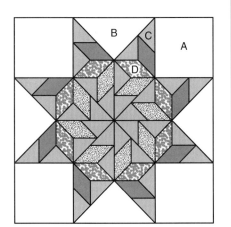

Fabric	Piece	Cut
1	C	8 squares, each 3¼" x 3¼"; cut twice diagonally for small quarter-square triangles
2	D	8 diamonds from a 1½"-wide strip
4	D	8 diamonds from a 1½"-wide strip
5	D	8 diamonds from a 1½"-wide strip
6	A	4 squares, each 4" x 4"
	B	1 square, 6¼" x 6"; cut twice diagonally for large quarter-square triangles

Piecing

Mark the ¼" seam intersections on all pieces. Matching the ¼" marks, sew the pieces together in numerical order. Stitch from the marks in the direction of the arrows as indicated in the illustrations.

When sewing the pieces together for this block, use a scant ¼"-wide seam allowance to ensure that the block will finish to 12".

Diamond Units

1. Sew a Fabric #2 and a Fabric #5 diamond (D) to the sides of a Fabric #1 triangle (C). Match the points of the diamonds and stitch. Trim the tips of the diamonds that extend beyond the seam allowances. Press the seams of the diamonds to one side and the seams of the triangle toward the diamonds. Press the seams of the diamonds in the same direction around the block.

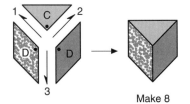

Make 8

2. Sew a Fabric #4 diamond (D) and 3 small Fabric #1 triangles (C) to the unit made in step 1 to complete the diamond unit.

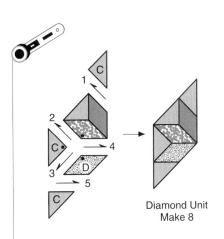

Diamond Unit
Make 8

Block Assembly

Arrange the diamonds, side triangles (B), and corner squares (A) as shown. Sew the units together, following the directions on pages 6–7 for constructing an eight-pointed star.

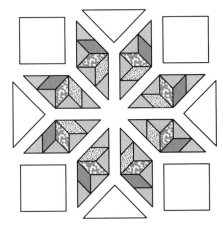

CASTLE KEEP

Cutting

Fabric	Piece	Cut
1	F	1 strip, 2" x 42"
2	F	1 strip, 2" x 42"
3	E	2 squares, each 6¼" x 6¼"; cut twice diagonally for quarter-square triangles
5	A	1 square, 5½" x 5½"
6	B	4 squares, each 2" x 2"
	C	6 squares, each 2⅜" x 2⅜"; cut twice diagonally for quarter-square triangles
	D	2 squares, each 4⅜" x 4⅜"; cut once diagonally for half-square triangles

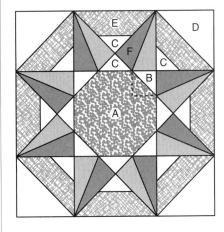

Piecing

Center Unit

Mark a diagonal line on the wrong side of each small background square (B). Place a marked square on a corner of the large Fabric #5 square (A). Stitch on the diagonal line and trim the seam allowance to ¼". Press the triangle toward the corner. Repeat with the remaining marked squares on the other 3 corners of the large square.

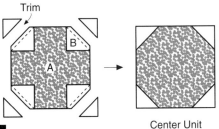

Center Unit
Make 1

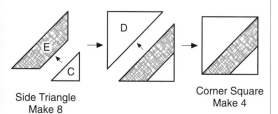

Side Triangle
Make 8

Corner Square
Make 4

Side Triangles and Corner Squares

1. To make a trapezoid (E), place the ruler's 2" mark on the long edge of a Fabric #3 quarter-square triangle. Use a rotary cutter to trim the corner.

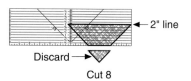

← 2" line

Discard →

Cut 8

2. Sew a small background triangle (C) to the short side of a Fabric #3 trapezoid (E). To each of 4 E/C units, sew a large background triangle (D) to make a corner square. Press the seams toward the trapezoid. Use the remaining 4 (E/C) units for the side triangles.

Side Units

1. With right sides together, sew the Fabric #1 and Fabric #2 strips together on both long edges using a ¼"-wide seam allowance.

2. Make a paper template of the Castle Keep cutting guide on page 43; mark the grain line and seam lines (see page 5). Place the corner of the template on the underside corner of a ruler; tape in place.

3. With the wrong side of the Fabric #2 strip face up, place the edge of the template on one edge of the strip unit. Cut along both edges of the ruler. To cut the next segment, rotate the ruler so that the edge of the template is on the opposite long edge of the strip unit; trim. Continue rotating the ruler from one long edge to the other to cut 6 more segments.

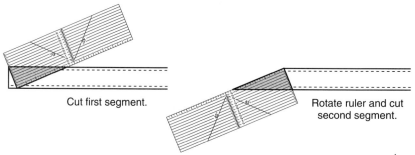

Cut first segment.

Rotate ruler and cut
second segment.

4. Carefully undo the stitching at the point of each segment. Press the seam open and trim away any tips extending beyond the edge.

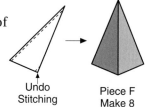

Undo
Stitching

Piece F
Make 8

5. Sew a side triangle (C/E unit) to the Fabric #1 side of Piece F.

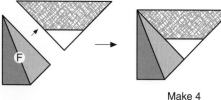

Make 4

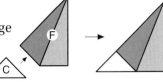

6. Sew the short side of a background triangle (C) to the Fabric #2 short edge of Piece F.

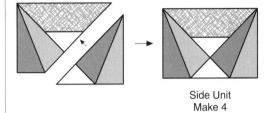

Make 4

7. Sew the units made in steps 5 and 6 together to complete the side units.

Side Unit
Make 4

Block Assembly

Arrange the center unit, side units, and corner squares as shown. Sew the units together in horizontal rows. Join the rows to complete the block.

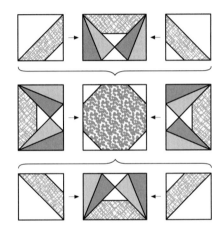

TWINKLING STAR

Cutting

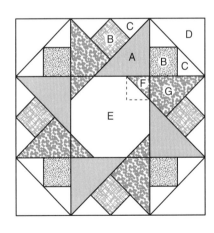

Fabric	Piece	Cut	
1	A	2 squares, each 4⅜" x 4⅜"; cut once diagonally for half-square triangles	
3	B	4 squares, each 2¼" x 2¼"	
4	B	4 squares, each 2¼" x 2¼"	
5	F	4 squares, each 2" x 2"	
	G	2 squares, each 4⅜" x 4⅜"; cut once diagonally for half-square triangles	
6	C	4 squares, each 3¾" x 3¾"; cut twice diagonally for quarter-square triangles	
	D	2 squares, each 4⅜" x 4⅜"; cut once diagonally for half-square triangles	
	E	1 square, 5½" x 5½"	

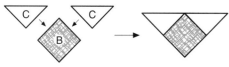

Piecing

Side Units

1. Sew the short side of two background triangles (C) to a Fabric #3 square (B).

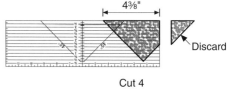

2. To cut Piece G, place the corner of a ruler on a Fabric #5 triangle (G) so that the ruler's 4⅜" mark is on the left-hand point of the triangle and the top edge of the ruler is even with the top of the triangle. Cut along the edge of the ruler to trim the corner of the triangle.

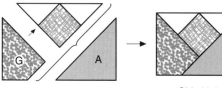

3. Sew Fabric #5 Piece G to the left side of a unit made in step 1. Sew this unit to a large Fabric #1 triangle (A).

Corner Squares

Sew the short side of 2 background triangles (C) to a Fabric #4 square (B). Sew this unit to a large background triangle (D).

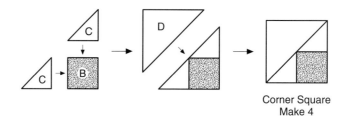

Center Unit

Mark a diagonal line on the wrong side of each small Fabric #5 square (F). Place a marked square on a corner of the large background square (E). Stitch on the diagonal line and trim the seam allowance to ¼". Press the triangle toward the corner. Repeat with the remaining marked squares on the other 3 corners of the large square.

Block Assembly

Arrange the center unit, side units, and corner squares as shown. Sew the units together in horizontal rows. Join the rows to complete the block.

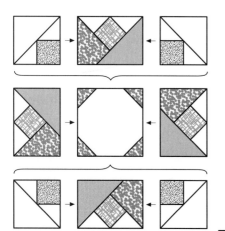

FEATHERED STAR

Cutting

Cut diamonds from strips, following directions on page 4.

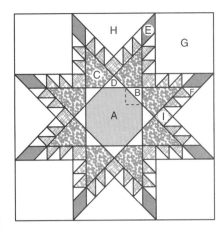

Fabric	Piece	Cut	
1	A	1 square, 3⅞" x 3⅞"	
2	E	8 diamonds from 1¼"-wide strips	
3	I	8 squares, each 1¼" x 1¼"	
	Triangle Units	1 piece, 6" x 22"	
5	C	4 squares, each 3¼" x 3¼"; cut once diagonally for half-square triangles	
6	B	4 squares, each 1½" x 1½"	
	D	2 squares, each 1⅞" x 1⅞"; cut once diagonally for half-square triangles	
	F	8 squares, each 1⅝" x 1⅝"; cut once diagonally for half-square triangles	
	G	4 squares, each 4" x 4"	
	H	1 square, 6¼" x 6¼"; cut twice diagonally for quarter-square triangles	
	Triangle Units	1 piece, 6" x 22"	

Half-Square Triangle Units for Feathers

1. Pair a 6" x 22" background and a Fabric #3 piece together with right sides facing up. Draw a true bias line on the top fabric, using a ruler with a 45°-angle line. Cut 7 bias strips parallel to the drawn line, each 1½" wide.

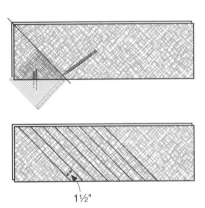

2. Sew the pairs of strips together along the bias edges, offsetting the tops of the strips ¼" as shown. Alternating the fabrics, sew the strips into two units, one with 8 strips and one with 6 strips. The smaller units are easier to work with than one long strip unit with all 14 strips.

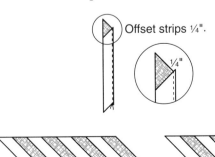

Offset strips ¼".

¼"

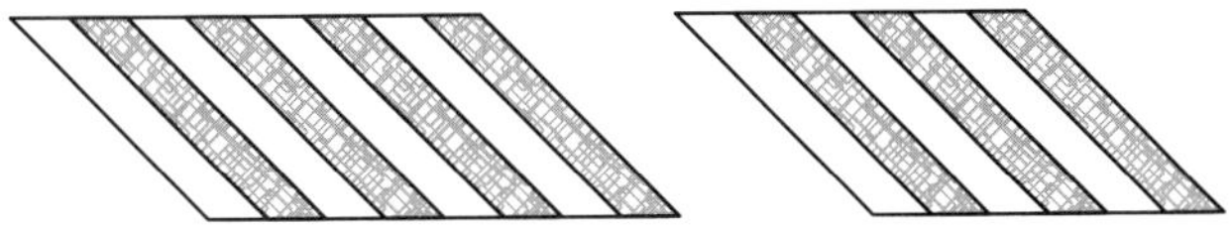

3. Place the diagonal line of the Bias Square® ruler on a seam line and a long ruler across the top to cut an even edge. Trim the edge; the trimmed edge should be at a perfect 45° angle to the seam lines. Cut 3 strips parallel to the straight edge, each 1¼" wide. Be sure to check and correct the angle at the edge after each cut.

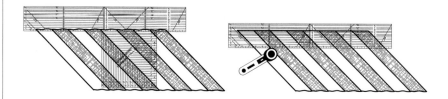

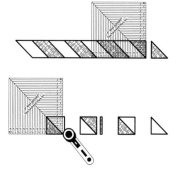

4. Place the diagonal line of the Bias Square ruler on a seam line and the bottom edge of the ruler on the cut edge of the strip. Cut on the right side of the ruler. Continue cutting across the strip from right to left. Rotate the pieces 180°, place the diagonal line of the Bias Square ruler on the seam line, and cut the second side to make a perfect square. Cut a total of 32 half-square triangle units.

Piecing

Mark the ¼" seam intersections on all pieces. Matching the ¼" marks, sew the pieces together in numerical order. Stitch from the marks in the direction of the arrows as indicated in the illustrations.

When sewing this block together, use a scant ¼"-wide seam allowance.

Corner Units

Arrange 4 half-square triangle units, 1 Fabric #3 square (I), 2 small background triangles (F), and 2 diamonds (E) on 2 sides of a large background square (G) as shown to complete the corner unit. Notice the position of the fabrics in the half-square triangle units. Sew the pieces together, following the piecing diagram. Press the seams toward the background square.

Side Units

1. Arrange 4 half-square triangle units, 1 Fabric #3 square (I), and 2 small background triangles (F) on the 2 short sides of a large background triangle (H). Notice the position of the fabrics in the half-square triangle units. Make 2 rows, following the piecing diagram.

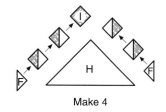

Make 4

2. Sew the short row to the right side of the triangle. Stitch from the edge in the direction of the arrow and stop in the middle of the background triangle (F). Sew the long row to the left side in the same manner. Press the seams toward the background triangle. Sewing a half seam in this manner is called half-seam construction and is used to avoid sewing a set-in seam. The seam will be finished when the corner units and side units are joined.

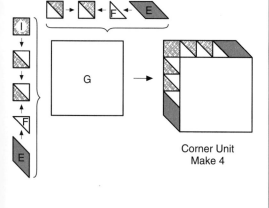

Corner Unit
Make 4

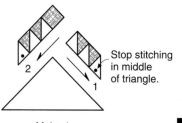

Stop stitching in middle of triangle.

Make 4

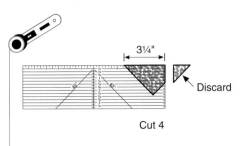

Cut 4

3. To cut Piece C, place the corner of a ruler on a Fabric #5 triangle (C) so that the 3¼" mark on the ruler is on the left-hand point of the triangle and the top edge of the ruler is even with the top of the triangle. Cut along the edge of the ruler to trim the corner of the triangle.

Discard

4. Sew Piece C to the left side of the unit made in step 2.

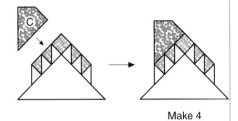

Make 4

5. Sew a small background triangle (D) to Piece C. Make 4. Sew this unit to the right side of the unit made in step 4 to complete the side unit.

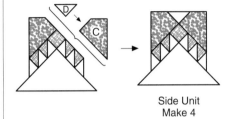

Side Unit
Make 4

Center Unit

Mark a diagonal line on the wrong side of each small background square (B). Place a marked square on a corner of the large Fabric #1 square (A). Stitch on the diagonal line and trim the seam allowance to ¼". Press the triangle toward the corner. Repeat with the remaining marked squares on the other 3 corners of the large square.

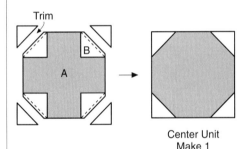

Center Unit
Make 1

Block Assembly

1. Arrange the units as shown.

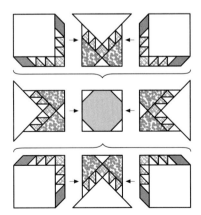

2. Sew the units together in horizontal rows. Sew the side of the corner unit to the side unit first, matching the ¼" marks. Stop stitching at the ¼" mark on the diamond. Then finish the remainder of the half seam along the large triangle. Join the rows to complete the block.

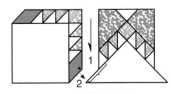

Finish half seam.

QUILT TOP ASSEMBLY AND FINISHING

STARS GALORE MEDALLION SETTING

You will need 13 star blocks for this setting. Color photo is on the cover. Quilt plan and yardage requirements are on page 8.

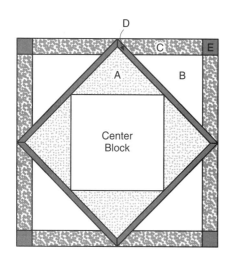

Center Medallion

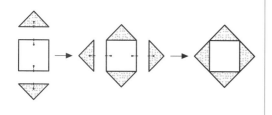

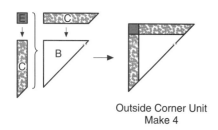

Outside Corner Unit
Make 4

Cutting

Fabric	Piece	Cut
5	C	8 strips, each 2½" x 11½"
6	B	2 squares, each 9⅝" x 9⅝"; cut once diagonally for half-square triangles
Center Background	A	2 squares, each 9⅜" x 9⅜"; cut once diagonally for half-square triangles
Sashing	D	4 strips, 1⅛" x 19¼"
Cornerstone	E	4 squares, each 2½" x 2½"

Piecing

Center Unit

1. Sew the 4 large medallion triangles (A) to the Feathered Star block. Fold the block in half and place a pin at the center point; fold the triangle in half and place a pin at the center point of the long side. Matching the center pins, stitch the triangles to the block.

2. Fold sashing strips (D) in half crosswise and make a mark at the center point. Pin the sashing strip to the side of the center unit, matching the center mark on the sashing to the corners of the block. Stitch each sashing in place and miter the corners. (See steps 6 and 7 on page 38.) The unfinished size of the center unit should be 18½" x 18½".

Outside Corner Units

1. Layer 2 Fabric #5 strips (C) with wrong sides together and cut a 45° angle at one end. Repeat with remaining strips. Make sure you cut precisely at the corner. The long side of the strip should still measure 11½".

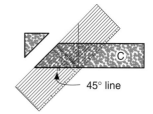

45° line

2. Sew the strips (C) trimmed in step 1 and a cornerstone (E) to the short sides of a background triangle (B) to make an outside corner unit.

3. Fold the corner units in half and mark the center of the long edge with a pin. Matching the center pin on the corner unit to the center mark of the sashing strip (D), sew the corner units to the center square in numerical order.

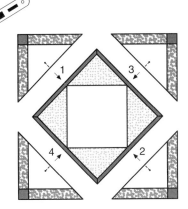

Setting the Blocks

From fabric for sashing, cut:
    36 strips, each 2½" x 12½"
From fabric for cornerstones, cut:
    24 squares, each 2½" x 2½"

1. Arrange the blocks around the center medallion as shown.

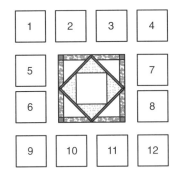

2. Sew 4 sashing strips and 5 cornerstones together to make a sashing row. Make 4 sashing rows.

Sashing Row
Make 4

3. Sew the top row of blocks and 5 sashing strips together. Sew this row between 2 sashing rows. Repeat with the bottom row of blocks.

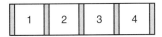

4. Sew a sashing strip to opposite sides of the remaining 4 blocks.

5. Sew a cornerstone to oppposite ends of a sashing strip. Sew this unit between 2 blocks to make a side block unit.

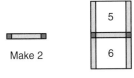

Make 2

Make 2

6. Sew the side block units made in step 5 to each side of the center medallion.

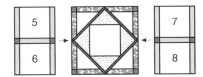

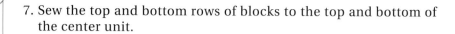

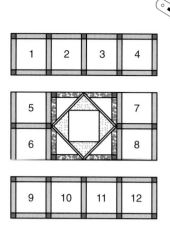

7. Sew the top and bottom rows of blocks to the top and bottom of the center unit.

Adding the Inner Border
From fabric for inner border, cut:
   8 strips, each 1¼" x 42"

1. Sew 2 strips together end to end to make one long strip. Make 4 long border strips.

2. Measure the length and width of the quilt through the center and note the measurements.

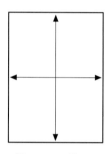

Measure quilt top
without borders.

3. Fold the quilt in half and mark the centers of the quilt edges. Fold each border strip in half and mark each center with a pin.
4. Place a pin at each end of the side border strips to mark the length of the quilt top. Repeat with the top and bottom borders.

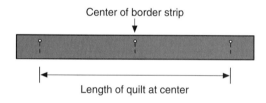

Center of border strip

Length of quilt at center

5. Pin the border strips to the quilt top, matching the centers. Line up the pins at either end of the border strip with the edges of the quilt. Stitch, beginning and ending the stitching ¼" from the corners of the quilt top.

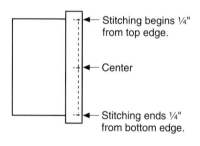

Stitching begins ¼" from top edge.

Center

Stitching ends ¼" from bottom edge.

6. Place a corner of the quilt on the ironing board, right side up, and pin in place. Fold under a strip at a 45° angle; pin and press. Center a strip of 1"-wide masking tape over the mitered fold, removing the pins as you go. Remove quilt from ironing board.

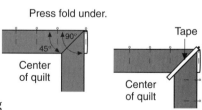

Press fold under.

Center of quilt

Tape

Center of quilt

7. On the wrong side, fold the quilt as shown and draw a stitching line on the border. Stitch on the line and remove the masking tape from the right side. Trim away excess border, leaving a ¼"-wide seam allowance beyond the stitching. Press the seam open. Repeat with remaining corners.

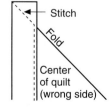

Stitch

Fold

Center of quilt (wrong side)

Adding the Middle Pieced Border

See page 8 for border yardage requirements.

From light background, cut:
   12 strips, each 2" x 42"
From medium background, cut:
   12 strips, each 2" x 42"
From diamond #1, cut:
   6 strips, each 2" x 42"
From diamond #2, cut:
   6 strips, each 2" x 42"

1. Sew the strips together, staggering the ends about 2" as shown to make 4 different strip units. Make 3 of each color combination.

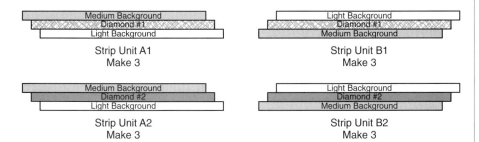

2. Layer strip unit A1 and B2 with right sides together, aligning the staggered ends. The same background strips should face each other, and the middle diamond strips should be different from each other. With the 45° line of your ruler on a horizontal seam line, trim the staggered end at a 45° angle. Cut 2"-wide segments from each pair of strip units, making your cuts parallel to the first cut. Keep the pairs of segments together. Check the angle of the cut edge after every 3 or 4 cuts to make sure it is at a true 45°; trim again if necessary. Repeat with strip units A2 and B1, cutting the 45° angle and segments in the opposite direction. Cut 14 segments from each pair of strip units.

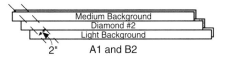

3. Sew the pairs of segments together. Always stitch from the tip of the background #2 diamond to the opposite end as shown.

B2/A1   B1/A2

4. For each border strip, sew 10 B2/A1 segments together and 10 A2/B1 segments together. Join the 2 sets of joined segments so that the #2 diamonds meet in the center. Trim each long side of the border strip, leaving a ¼"-wide seam allowance beyond the diamond points. Place the ruler's ¼" mark on the diamond points and use your rotary cutter to trim along the edges of the ruler. Make 4 border strips.

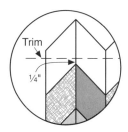

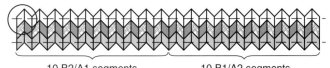

10 B2/A1 segments   10 B1/A2 segments

39

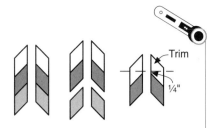

Trim
¼"

5. To make the corner units, cut 4 additional segments, each 2" wide, from strip unit A2 and 4 from B2 for a total of 8. Remove the bottom diamond (background #2) and trim the top diamond, leaving a ¼"-wide seam allowance above the tip of the diamond.

6. From background #1 fabric, cut 4 squares, each 2½" x 2½". Sew 2 diamond units from step 5 to the sides of a 2½" background square.

Corner Unit
Make 4

7. Sew a pieced border strip to the top and bottom edges of the quilt. The edges of the border strips are on the bias so be careful not to stretch them. Center the 2 dark diamonds in the middle of the border strip on the center of each side. Add a corner unit to each end of the remaining pieced border strips and sew to the sides of the quilt, again centering the 2 dark diamonds on the center of each side.

Center 2 dark diamonds here and on opposite side.

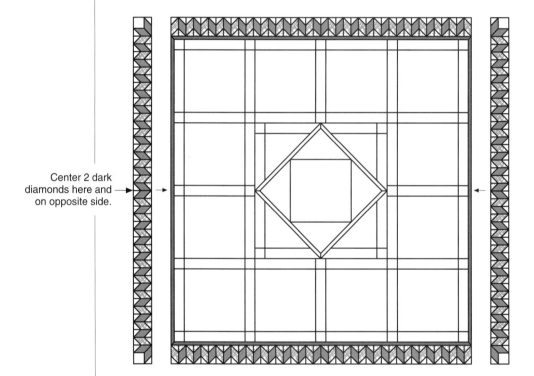

Adding the Outer Border

From the fabric for the outer border, cut 8 strips, each 4½" x 42". Sew the outer border to the quilt top, following directions on page 38 for the inner border.

Quilt Finishing

1. Layer the quilt top with batting and backing; baste.
2. Quilt as desired.
3. Bind the edges of the quilt.
4. Sign and date your quilt.

EIGHT STARS ON POINT SETTING

You will need 8 star blocks for this setting. Color photo is on page 21. Quilt plan and yardage requirements are on page 9.

Cutting and Piecing

From fabric for sashing, cut:

8 strips, each 3" x 42; crosscut into 24 segments, each 3" x 12½"

From fabric for cornerstones, cut:

2 strips, each 3" x 42"; crosscut into 17 squares, each 3" x 3"

From fabric for setting triangles, cut:

2 squares, each 21½" x 21½"; cut twice diagonally to yield 8 side triangles; you will only use 6.

2 squares, each 13" x 13"; cut once diagonally to yield 4 corner triangles

1. Arrange the blocks on point. Position the sashing strips and cornerstones around the blocks. Sew the sashing strips between the blocks and at the end of each row. Sew the sashing strips and cornerstones together to make sashing rows.

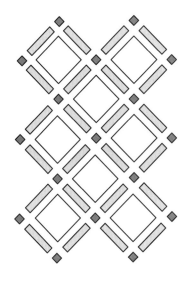

2. Sew the sashing rows and rows of blocks together. Add the side triangles to the ends of the rows.

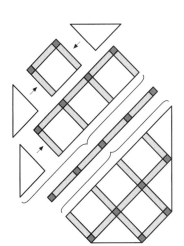

3. Join the rows and add the corner triangles last.

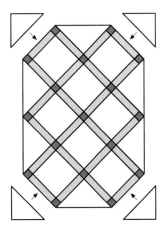

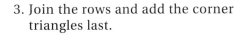

Adding the Inner Border

From fabric for inner border, cut:
    7 strips, each 3¼" x 42"

1. Cut 1 of the border strips in half. Sew a half strip to one end of 2 of the 42"-long strips to make the top and bottom border strips. Sew 2 more strips together to make 2 pieced side border strips. See step 1 on page 38 for joining strips.
2. Sew the pieced inner border strips to the quilt top, following directions on page 38 for adding borders and mitering corners.

Adding the Pieced Border

From background #1, cut:
    12 strips, each 2¼" x 42"
From background #2, cut:
    12 strips, each 2¼" x 42"
From diamond #1, cut:
    6 strips, each 2¼" x 42"
From diamond #2, cut:
    6 strips, each 2¼" x 42"

1. Follow the directions on pages 39–40 for the Star Medallion pieced border to cut and assemble the strip units. Cut 12 segments, each 2¼" wide, from each pair of strip units.

2. For the top and bottom borders, sew 7 pairs of segments together from each strip unit. Join the 2 sets of joined segments together, making sure the center diamonds are the same color. Make 2 pieced borders. Sew borders to top and bottom edges of quilt.

3. For the side borders, sew 10 pairs of segments together from each strip unit. Join the 2 sets of joined segments together, making sure the center diamonds are the same color. Make 2 pieced side borders.

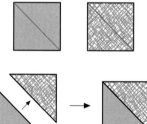

4. Follow steps 5 and 6 on page 40 to make the corner units, but instead of cutting a plain square for the corner, make a pieced half-square triangle unit. Cut 2 squares, each 3⅜" x 3⅜", from background #2 and 2 from diamond #1 fabrics (for a total of 4 squares). Cut the squares once diagonally and sew 2 different triangles together on the bias edge (long edge).

5. Sew corner units to each end of remaining pieced borders. Sew to sides of quilt.

Adding the Outer Border

From the fabric for the outer border, cut 8 strips, each 2½" x 42". Sew 2 of the strips together to make 1 long strip. Make 4 pieced border strips. Sew the outer borders to the quilt top in the same manner as the inner border.

Quilt Finishing

1. Layer the quilt top with batting and backing; baste.
2. Quilt as desired.
3. Bind the edges of the quilt.
4. Sign and date your quilt.

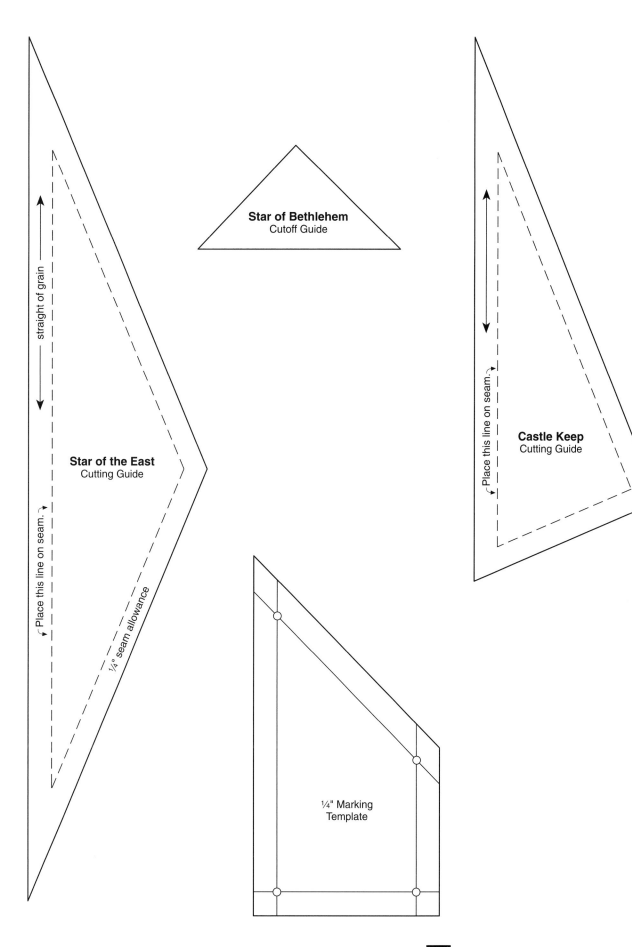

Star of Bethlehem
Cutoff Guide

straight of grain

Star of the East
Cutting Guide

Place this line on seam.

¼" seam allowance

Castle Keep
Cutting Guide

Place this line on seam.

¼" Marking
Template

ABOUT THE AUTHOR

Roxanne Carter is a prolific quiltmaker, producing ten quilts a year and teaching three to four classes per month. She learned to sew from her mom at the age of five and was making her own clothes by high school. It was quiltmaking, however, that really ignited her creative spark. She has been teaching quilting classes for the past five years in local quilt shops and to Seattle-area guilds.

Her enthusiasm for quilting is contagious and is eagerly shared by her husband, Rob, a quiltmaker and woodworker. He organizes all of her teaching materials and is responsible for all of her advertising. More than fifty of their quilts are periodically displayed in local quilt shops or adorn the walls and grace the beds of their home in Mukilteo, Washington. In addition to Rob, two children and two wonderful grand-children share in Roxanne's enthusiasm for the art of quiltmaking.